Acting Edition

Alice in Wonderland

by Brainerd Duffield

From the story by Lewis Carroll

ALICE IN WONDERLAND

A Three-Act Play With Fourteen Adventures

For Twenty or More Characters

CHARACTERS

ALICE

WHITE RABBIT

QUEEN OF HEARTS

MOUSE

CATERPILLAR

FROG FOOTMAN

FISH FOOTMAN

DUCHESS

DORMOUSE

MARCH HARE

MAD HATTER

GRYPHON

MOCK TURTLE

KING OF HEARTS

KNAVE OF HEARTS

RED QUEEN

TWEEDLEDUM

TWEEDLEDEE

WHITE QUEEN

HUMPTY DUMPTY

EXTRAS

HERALDS
PAGES
HUNTSMEN
PLAYING CARDS
And others as desired

NOTES ON DOUBLING

The following characters appear in one act only; thus a single actor can play one appropriate role from each column.

ACT I	ACT II
Mouse	2 of Spades
Caterpillar	5 of Spades
Frog Footman	7 of Spades
Fish Footman	Gryphon
Duchess	Mock Turtle
Cook	Knave of Hearts

ACT III
Red Queen
White Queen
Tweedledum
Tweedledee
Humpty Dumpty

All of the above can be fitted with alternate costumes as Pages and Heralds to the Queen of Hearts, to fill out crowd scenes.

The following characters should not be doubled:

Alice
White Rabbit
Queen of Hearts
Dormouse
March Hare
Mad Hatter

Cast size may range from twenty to fifty.

Additional notes on the cast are in the back of this book.

ALICE IN WONDERLAND ADVENTURES
SYNOPSIS OF SCENES

ACT I

ACT II

ACT III

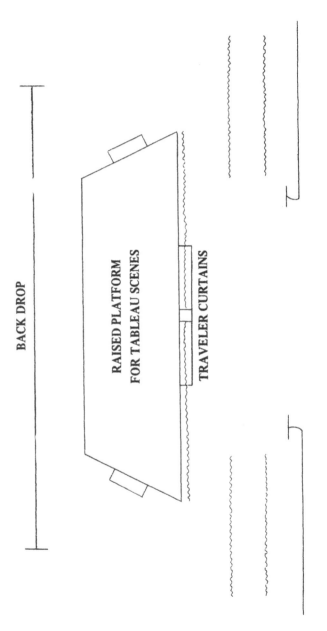

BACK DROP

RAISED PLATFORM
FOR TABLEAU SCENES

TRAVELER CURTAINS

SCENE DESIGN

See back pages for production notes.

ALICE IN WONDERLAND

ACT I

Adventure 1: Down the rabbit hole.

AT RISE OF CURTAIN: ALICE is seated facing front on
the upstage tableau platform, supposedly on a grassy bank with
clumps of flowers here and there. She has a book in her hand
and her back is against a tree. The area glows with amber,
indicating a summer's day and there is a blue sky behind her.
ALICE turns a page in her book, but seems on the verge of
dozing off. If taped or recorded music is used, a selection by
Delius, such as In A Summer Garden, would make a suitable
background for the following speech.

ALICE. *[Sleepily]* What a very warm day it is, and what a
 boring book this is! It has no pictures and what's the use
 of a book like that? . . . Hot days make me feel stupid,
 though I'm considered very bright for my age. Everyone
 says so.

 *[Her head nods forward and she closes her eyes. She
 awakens and looks up as the WHITE RABBIT enters
 from wings. ALICE rises and follows him.]*

RABBIT. Oh, dear! Oh, dear! I'm going to be late. The
 Duchess will be furious. *[He takes a watch from his
 pocket and squints at it.]* I'm supposed to escort her
 to the palace garden for the Queen of Hearts' croquet
 tournament. If we're late for **that**, the Queen is bound

to chop off our heads. *[During the speech, he has crossed the stage to pause DR.]* That's the penalty for being late.

[He pockets his watch and exits to wings DR.]

ALICE. Oh, dear! I've seen quite a few rabbits, but never one that took a watch from his pocket. *[Peering offstage]* He must have gone down that rabbit hole. Quite a large rabbit hole. Big enough for **me**. I'll risk it.

[She exits DR as all lights fade out. During the blackout, the traveler curtains close in front of the rear tableau platform. A spotlight with a multicolored pinwheel picks out ALICE at midstage C. As it whirls, she gyrates to L and R with arms upraised, giving an illusion of falling through space. Dream music is played during the following speech.]

ALICE. Help! I don't want to fall! Help! Catch me! O-o-o-o! *[Relaxing]* O-o-o! I wonder how many miles I've fallen by this time. I may fall right **through** the earth! How funny it would be to see people walking upside down. I shall ask: 'Please, ma'am, is this New Zealand or Australia? *[The color pinwheel slows to a stop and ALICE sits down with a thump, legs asprawl.]* I seem to have reached the bottom! Or mine at any rate! *[The spotlight holds on ALICE as she gets to her feet and brushes off her skirt. The rest of the stage remains dark, as another spot picks out a small gold table against the black curtain DL. On the table is a bottle with a large tag attached. ALICE crosses DL and picks up the bottles and reads the tag.]* It says: 'DRINK ME.' It's **not** marked 'poison' – so I'll taste it. Very nice. It has a mixed flavor of cherry-tart, custard, pineapple, roast turkey, and hot buttered toast. Delicious. *[She finishes drinking the bottle, puts the stopper back in. A black gloved arm reaches from the wings and takes the bottle from her*

*hand. Eerie music is heard. The table, drawn by unseen wires
above, begins to rise slowly into the air. ALICE hugs herself
with her arms and fearfully watches as the table disappears
into the darkness above.]* Good heavens, I must be shrinking.
I don't feel more than two feet high. Oh, dear!

*[The general lighting brightens somewhat and a spotlight
picks out the RABBIT, as he reappears DR. He stops, con-
sults his watch, and shakes it vigorously.]*

ALICE. Here's that nice rabbit again. *[She starts to intercept
him.]* Oh, sir! I seem to have lost my way. And I have the
horrible feeling I've been shrinking. You look much larger
than the last time I saw you. *[The RABBIT'S back is to
ALICE and he pays no attention to her.]*
RABBIT. Oh, my ears and whiskers! I'll have to go back to
the house. I forgot my gloves. The Duchess wil be beside
herself with fury, and the Queen of Hearts will certainly
chop off my head. She'll make rabbit stew of me and put me
into a pie.

*[He patters off again DR in the direction from which he
had come, leaving ALICE forlorn at DC. ALICE takes a
step or two after him, holding out a beseeching hand.
Sound: A blare of trumpets is heard.]*

VOICES. *[Offstage L]* Make way for Her Majesty! Make way
for the Queen of Hearts!

*[Another fanfair. Martial music. Enter the QUEEN OF
HEARTS and her royal retinue. HERALDS and PAGES
precede her. These are playing card characters and wear
white sandwich boards emblazoned with hearts and
numerals. She is followed by playing card HUNTSMEN
with bows and arrows, and an EXECUTIONER with a*

*black hood over his head with slits for eyes. He carries a
large axe.]*

QUEEN OF HEARTS. *[Loudly]* Off with their heads! *[The
entourage has halted ULC and the QUEEN steps forward
to point an imperious finger at ALICE.]* Who is **this**?
Who is this person? How dare you enter my domain!
What is your name, you horrid little girl?

ALICE. *[Making a curtsey]* My name is Alice, so please Your
Majesty. At least it **was** when I got up this morning. *[In-
timidated by the QUEEN'S angry tone, ALICE has backed
away a step or two.]*

QUEEN. *[Suddenly affable]* So your name is Alice. I'm very
fond of Alices. You must come to my garden this afternoon
and play croquet.

ALICE. Thank you, Your Majesty! *[Curtsies]*

QUEEN. I'm baking tarts for the occasion from my royal
recipe.

ALICE. Lovely. I'm very fond of tarts. At tea time, my
mother always scolds me for helping myself.

QUEEN. *[Angry]* You had better not help yourself to **my**
tarts! Stealing tarts is a capital offense! I always have an
executioner close by to behead anyone caught stealing
tarts! *[The EXECUTIONER raises his axe menacingly.]*

ALICE. *[Shrinking away]* Oh, please don't behead me, Your
Majesty! Such strange things have been happening and
I'm very anxious to get back home and see Dinah. She's
my cat.

QUEEN. *[Outraged]* Impossible! Only royal persons are
permitted to go home. You'll have to become a queen
yourself before you'll be allowed to go!

ALICE. *[Astounded]* I shall have to become Queen Alice?
Just to leave?

QUEEN. Certainly, you foolish girl! And you'll have **many**
strange adventures before that happens. Every adventure

is a necessary step. First, you must journey across Wonderland, until you come to the border of Looking-Glass Land. Then, you must travel square by square on the **giant chessboard** until you get to the eighth row. **Then**, you will be a Queen yourself and may go anywhere you please.

ALICE. *[Sighing]* It sounds very difficult and confusing.

QUEEN. *[Vindictively]* You had no business coming here in the first place!

ALICE. Yes, ma'am, and I never shall again.

QUEEN. Hold your tongue! I'm a hungry hyena, and you're a bone!

ALICE. *[Very frightened]* I beg your royal pardon!

QUEEN. You'd better, or I'll have your head chopped off! Come to the croquet game this afternoon. Mind your manners when you get there, and don't be late, or you'll be punished.

HERALD. *[Pointing off R]* Tallyho!

QUEEN. *[Shouts]* Tallyho! Off with their heads! Tallyho!

[She exits R, trotting briskly, followed by her pages and guards, some brandishing swords and spears. The EX-ECUTIONER brings up the rear with his axe held high. ALICE crosses UC with a frightened expression. She takes a handkerchief from her apron pocket and dabs at the perspiration on her brow.]

ALICE. *[Breathlessly]* And she tells **me** to mind **my** manners!

QUEEN. *[Heard at a distance]* Off with their heads! Off with their heads!

CHORUS OF VOICES. *[Heard offstage L]* Tallyho! Tallyho! *[This is followed by screams.]*

ALICE. How very curious everything is today!

[The WHITE RABBIT returns from the wings DR. He is in a great hurry, glancing back over his shoulder. He carries a pair of white gloves in one hand and a fan in the other.]

ALICE. Mister Rabbit, sir!

RABBIT. *[Startled, he faces her.]* Oh, it's **you** again! You've met the Queen of Hearts, have you? I'll wager you're sorry now that you followed me here. Did she ask you to play croquet?

ALICE. Yes, she did — and very discourteously.

RABBIT. I shouldn't go, if I were you. It's very dangerous to play games with Her Majesty.

ALICE. She threatened to **punish** me severely, if I **didn't** go.

RABBIT. She will. Her Majesty has a dreadful temper.

QUEEN OF HEARTS. *[Heard from afar]* Off with their heads, I say! *[Screams of peasants faintly heard.]*

ALICE. *[Worried]* I was told not to be late, but she didn't say what **time** the croquet match began.

RABBIT. Get there as soon as you can. The Queen will decide for herself whether you're late or not.

ALICE. I shall start crying any minute. Please, could you tell me —

RABBIT. No time! No time! Oh, the Duchess! Won't she be savage, if I've kept her waiting.

QUEEN OF HEARTS. *[Offstage R, loudly and much closer]* Off with their heads!

RABBIT. *[Startled, leaps in air dropping gloves]* No time! No time! No time!

[He scampers off DL, muttering nervously.]

ALICE. *[Picking them up]* Sir, you've dropped your gloves. *[She begins to cry.]* Oh, I'm so afraid and homesick. *[She wrings out the handkerchief, which conceals a small plastic bag and a wet sponge. Tears spill on floor.]* Stop crying! You ought to be ashamed of yourself, a big girl like you. Yesterday things were just as usual. I changed during the night. But if I'm not the same as I was, who am I? I'll see if I can remember a song I used to know. *[She sings.]*

How doth the little crocodile
Improve his shining tail,
And pour the waters of the Nile
On every golden scale.

How cheerfully he seems to grin,
How neatly spreads his claws,
And welcomes little fishes in
With gently smiling jaws!

ALICE. Oh, my! I'm sure those aren't the right words. *[She resumes her sobbing, and skates and skids about.]* I can't stop crying and it's so slippery underfoot. I'm wading in a puddle of tears. I'll be up to my chin in salt water. *[Sound of bubbling and splashing water. The lights go dark for a brief moment, as the sound effects build to a crescendo.]*

Adventure 2: The pool of tears.

[Lights – green and blue – illuminate the upstage tableau platform where the traveler curtians have been opened. Offstage to L and R and not seen by the audience are stagehands.   They hold lengths of scrimcloth or transparent green plastic between them to represent waves. This 'pool of water' should billow up and down, back and forth. It is raised from the floor to the level of ALICE'S chin. Upstage of the fabric, she pantomimes the motions of swiming back and forth.]

ALICE. Help! Help! Save me! . . . I'm drowning!

[A MOUSE swims into view from L, paddling with its forepaws and treading water.]

MOUSE. Stop complaining!

ALICE. Good gracious, a mouse. We'll both be drowned.
Mouse, do you know the way out of this pool? I am tired
of swimming. *[The MOUSE begins to swim more strenuously,
and the STAGEHANDS agitate the cloth back and forth to
indicate churning water.]* Oh, he won't listen. I know, I'll
call cat! Cat! *[The MOUSE leaps suddenly into the air,
quivering with fright.]* Oh, I beg your pardon!

MOUSE. *[Shrilly]* Would **you** like cats if you were me?

ALICE. Don't be angry. I wish I could show you Dinah. She's
such a dear, purring by the fire — and she's wonderful for
catching mice — oh, I beg your pardon! *[The MOUSE leaps
into the air again in great alarm.]* We won't talk about her
any more.

MOUSE. We, indeed! As if **I** would talk on such a subject!
Our family always **hated** cats: nasty, low, vulgar things!

ALICE. Are you — are you fond — of dogs? *[No answer from
MOUSE.]* There is such a nice dog, near our house, a terrier.
The farmer says it kills rats and — oh, dear! I'm afraid I've
offended it again!

*[The MOUSE swims vigorously out of view L. stirring a
great commotion of rippling water as it goes. ALICE calls
after it.]*

ALICE. Mouse dear! We won't talk about cats, or dogs either,
if you don't like them!

*[The MOUSE has performed an about face and swims back
into view and looks her in the eye.]*

MOUSE. *[In a trembling voice]* Let's get to the shore, then
I'll tell you my history. You'll understand why I hate cats
and dogs. *[ALICE and MOUSE swim to upstage end of
platform. There is a rock cutout behind the riser. Using a*

*concealed sponge, ALICE squeezes water from her skirt.
The two STAGEHANDS simply let their scrimcloth drop
to the ground.]*

ALICE. *[To MOUSE]* You promised to tell me your history.
You know . . . *[In a confidential whisper]* why you hate C's
and D's.

MOUSE. *[With a sigh and holding his tail in his hand]* Mine is
a long and sad tale.

ALICE. It is a long tail, certainly. But why do you call it sad?
*[The following may be either recited or set to a musical
accompaniment.]*

MOUSE   We lived beneath the mat,
         Warm and snug and fat.
         With but one woe and that
         Was the cat!

         To our joys a clog.
         In our eyes a fog.
         On our hearts a log
         Was the dog!

         When the cat's away,
         Then the mice will play.
         But, alas! One day;
         So they say
         Came the dog and cat,
         Hunting for a rat,
         Crushed the mice all flat,
         Each one as he sat,
         Underneath the mat,
         Warm and snug and fat.
         Think of that!

MOUSE. *[Severely to ALICE]* You are not attending!

ALICE. On the contrary, I was paying close attention. But you're so easily offended, you know!

MOUSE. *[Growling]* Grrr! You can't talk to me like that! I shall walk out! *[He moves UR.]*

ALICE. *[Calls after MOUSE]* Please come back.

MOUSE. Let this be a lesson to you, never to lose your temper!

[He exits.]

ALICE. I wish I knew what all this meant and I wish I had Dinah here. She'd get the mouse back again! And she's such a capital cat for catching mice. I'm sure she's the **best** cat in the world. *[She comes down off the platform and moves toward DC. The traveler curtains close behind her.]* Oh, my dear Dinah! I wonder if I shall ever see you again! I wonder if I can get away from this place . . . without having my head . . . *[Puts her hand to her throat and begins to cry again, but stops as she hears the sound of footsteps offstage]* Someone's coming . . . I wonder if it's Mouse to finish his story?

[The WHITE RABBIT enters from UR.]

ALICE. Oh, sir. I'm really desperate to get home. If you could only tell me the proper road to take –

RABBIT. *[Greatly flustered]* The Duchess! The Duchess! Oh, my dear paws! Oh, my fur and whiskers! She'll get me executed as sure as carrots are carrots. Where can I have dropped them? Where are they? Where are they? *[He is busily looking about on the ground. ALICE begins looking too, in an effort to help him. They bypass each other once or twice and then come face-to-face.]* Run home this minute and fetch me a pair of gloves! Quick now!

[He exits DL. ALICE follows part way and is picked out by a spotlight in the L area.]

ALICE. *[Taking gloves from pocket and waving them futilely]* Here they are, sir. If only I'd known what he was looking for. Wherever I go something peculiar is bound to happen . . . *[She is about to follow DL where the RABBIT made his exit, but her attention is distracted as a large mushroom rolls into view on a platform DR from behind the tormentor.]*

Adventure 3: Caterpillar on a mushroom.

[Seated on a huge mushroom is a large blue CATERPILLAR smoking a hookah. ALICE goes toward him, staring upward in amazement. After puffing some smoke, the CATERPILLAR calmly removes the stem of the hookah from its mouth.]

CATERPILLAR. Who are **you?**

ALICE. I – I hardly know right now. At least I thought I knew who I was this morning, but I keep changing.

CATERPILLAR. Explain yourself.

ALICE. I can't explain myself, because I'm not myself, you see.

CATERPILLAR. I **don't** see.

ALICE. Being so many different places in a day is bewildering. And being two different sizes is very confusing. Is that any clearer?

CATERPILLAR. Not a bit. Who are **you?**

ALICE. *[Irritated]* I think you ought to tell me who **you** are first.

CATERPILLAR. **Why?** *[ALICE turns and starts away.]* Come back! I've something important to say! *[ALICE turns back to face him.]* Keep your temper!

ALICE. *[Swallowing her anger]* Is that all?

CATERPILLAR. No. *[ALICE waits while the CATERPILLAR puffs on his hookah, then finally unfolds his arms and removes the hookah from his mouth.]* So you think you're changed, do you?

ALICE. Yes. I can't remember things as I used to —

CATERPILLAR. Can't remember **what** things?

ALICE. Well, I've tried to recite 'How doth the little busy bee,' but it all came out different!

CATERPILLAR. Repeat 'You are old Father William.' *[ALICE folds her hands and begins to recite. Or this could be set to music and sung.]*

ALICE   'You are old, Father William,' the young man said,
          'And your hair has become very white;
      And yet you incessantly stand on your head —
          Do you think, at your age, it is right?'

      'In my youth,' Father William replied to his son,
          'I feared it would injure the brain;
      But now that I'm perfectly sure I have none,
          Why, I do it again and again.'

      'You are old,' said the youth, 'one would hardly suppose
          That your eye was as steady as ever;
      Yet you balanced an eel on the end of your nose —
          What made you so awfully clever?'

      'I have answered one question, and that is enough,
          Said his father. 'Don't give yourself airs!
      Do you think I can listen all day to such stuff?
          Be off, or I'll kick you downstairs!'

CATERPILLAR. *[After a pause]* That is not said right.

ALICE. Not quite right, I'm afraid.

CATERPILLAR. It is wrong from beginning to end. *[Puffs on his hookah]* What size do you want to be?

ALICE. Well, I should like to be a **little** larger. Three inches is such a wretched height to be.

CATERPILLAR. *[Outraged]* It is a very good height indeed!

ALICE. *[Pathetically]* But I'm not used to it.

CATERPILLAR. If you're determined to grow taller or shorter, just break a little piece off the edge.

ALICE. *[Puzzled]* The edge of what?

CATERPILLAR. The mushroom, of course. It's a magic mushroom. Do as I say, girl. *[ALICE, with great hesitation, steps DR and breaks off a morsel from the rim of the mushroom. She looks at the particle with curiosity.]*

ALICE. This will make me larger or smaller?

CATERPILLAR. Whichever you like. All you have to do is nibble and make a wish.

ALICE. *[Skeptically]* I just nibble and wish? *[She is about to take a bite.]*

CATERPILLAR. *[Shouts]* Not **now**!!!

ALICE. *[Very startled]* But when? . . . **When?**

CATERPILLAR. *[Mysteriously]* When the time comes.

ALICE. When will the time come?

CATERPILLAR. *[Darkly]* You'll **know**. Now tell me where you're going.

ALICE. I'm going to the palace to play croquet with the Queen of Hearts. *[The CATERPILLAR begins to chuckle wickedly.]* What are you laughing at?

CATERPILLAR. *[Continues to laugh]* Oh, I wouldn't do **that**, if I were you! Not if you ever want to go home!

ALICE. *[Alarmed]* Why do you say that?

CATERPILLAR. *[Sinister]* Many who go to the palace never go home at all. They lose their heads over it. *[Chuckles]*

ALICE. *[In distress]* But I've done no harm to anyone!

CATERPILLAR. You'll be accused of **something** before the day is out, mark my words! Let me give you some advice. Before it's too late.

ALICE. Please do!
CATERPILLAR. When the time comes, use your wish! Use
your wish, my girl.

*[He puffs on his hookah as the platform with CATER-
PILLAR amd mushroom is pulled back into wings DR.]*

Adventure 4: The house of the Duchess.

*[ALICE is still at DRC, staring offstage where the CATER-
PILLAR has disappeared. Simultaneously, a flat is shoved
into view from the UL wing. It has a door painted on it with
a practical doorstep attached. The door will be opened, and
the step is necessary for the FROG FOOTMAN to sit down
on. He now enters from UL. The FISH FOOTMAN marches
on from UR carrying a letter almost as large as himself.
Seeing him, ALICE countercrosses to URC to watch the
proceedings. The FISH FOOTMAN approaches the FROG
FOOTMAN to present the enormous letter, monogrammed
with a large Q.]*

FISH FOOTMAN. For the Duchess. An invitation from the
Queen of Hearts to play croquet.
FROG FOOTMAN. *[Accepting it]* From the Queen of Hearts.
An invitation for the Duchess to play croquet.

*[They bow very low to each other. Having performed his
errand, the FISH FOOTMAN turns on his heel and marches
to R and exits. Upstage of him, ALICE watches his de-
parture.]*

FROG FOOTMAN. *[Scornfully]* Croquet! An invitation to
beheading is what that means! *[He stands the letter on
end and slides it into the wings UL. He then sits down*

*on the doorstep. From offstage, we hear a great clamor
and clatter: a baby crying, the rattle of pots and pans,
glass crashes and the smashing of dishware. It ceases as
abruptly as it has begun. Now ALICE moves tentatively
toward where the FROG FOOTMAN is sitting. He speaks
without looking at her, seeming to stare at the sky.]*
There's no sort of use in knocking, and that for **two**
reasons. **First**, because I'm on the same side of the door
as you are. **Secondly**, because they're making such a
noise inside no one could possibly hear you. *[Repeat
the same offstage pandemonium of sound. It sustains
for a few brief moments, then is cut off again abruptly.]*

ALICE. How am I to get in?

FROG FOOTMAN. *[Still staring at the sky]* There might be
some sense in your knocking if we had the door between
us. For instance, if you were inside you might knock and
I could let you **out**, you know.

ALICE. But how am I to get **in**?

FROG FOOTMAN. **Are** you to get in at all? That's the first
question, you know.

ALICE. It's really dreadful the way these creatures argue. It's
enough to drive one crazy!

FROG FOOTMAN. I shall sit here on and off for days and days.

ALICE. But what am I to do?

FROG FOOTMAN. Anything you like. *[He begins to whistle.]*

ALICE. Oh, there's no use in talking to him. He's perfectly
idiotic! I shall go round to the kitchen door.

*[She starts toward L to exit. Lights fade out. In the blackout,
the FROG FOOTMAN exits and the flat is removed. The
sound of the hubbub from the kitchen starts up again and
this time continues. When lights come on, the tableau stage
curtains have been opened on the kitchen scene. The DUCHESS
sits on a rocking chair with the BABY in her lap. To R is a
box-like stove where the COOK stands stirring a large pot of*

soup. She stops stirring only to dump in quantities of
pepper from an outsize shaker, sneezing loudly whenever
she does so. Facing front on the floor by the stove is a
lantern-like paper head of the CHESHIRE CAT with
the light turned on inside. Its eyes and grin are of tissue,
as in a jack-o-lantern. ALICE enters platform from UL.]

COOK. *[Sneezing]* Ah-**choo**! Ah-**choo**! *[The BABY'S wailing*
   is softer so the dialogue can be heard.]
ALICE. *[Cat's head blinks on and off.]* There is certainly too
   much pepper in that soup. *[Sneezes]* Ah-**choo**! Please tell
   me why your cat grins like that?
DUCHESS. *[Gruff voice]* It's a Cheshire Cat, that's why. — Have
   you never heard of the expression: 'grinning like a Chesire
   Cat?' —
ALICE. I didn't know that cats **could** grin.
DUCHESS. They all can and they all do.
ALICE. I don't know any that do.
DUCHESS. You don't know much and that's a fact.
BABY. *[Voice faked from offstage]* Ow-woo! Hoo-hoo!
DUCHESS. **Pig**! *[ALICE reacts with momentary anger until*
   she sees that the DUCHESS is addressing the BABY and not
   herself. Whacking the BABY] Take that and that and **that**,
   you little pig!
BABY. Wow-oo! Boo-hoo! A-wooo!
ALICE. **Must** you spank the baby?
DUCHESS. Yes! *[Does so some more]* Take that and **that**!
   [Suddenly the COOK puts down her spoon and begins to
   hurl crockery at the DUCHESS and ALICE. These props
   should be frisbies painted to represent plates. They sail
   safely over the heads of the DUCHESS and ALICE and
   into the wings UL where the crashing of glass is heard.
   Then things quiet down as the COOK returns to stirring
   the soup and the DUCHESS rocks the BABY.]

ALICE. I wish your cook wouldn't throw the plates around that way. She'll hurt the baby's precious nose!

DUCHESS. Not your business. If everybody minded their own business the world would go around a deal faster.

ALICE. *[Shrugs]* Which would not be an advantage. You see, the earth takes twenty-four hours to turn round on its axis . . .

DUCHESS. Talking of axes – **chop off his head!** *[ALICE glances anxiously at the COOK, who is too busy stirring soup to pay any attention.]*

ALICE. Or is it twelve?

DUCHESS. Oh, don't bother me! I never liked arithmetic. *[She begins singing to the BABY, giving it a violent shake at the end of each line.]*

DUCHESS 'Speak roughly to your little boy
        And beat him when he sneezes,
        He only does it to annoy
        Because he knows it teases.'

CHORUS *[The COOK and the BABY'S voice join in to sing.]*
        'Wow! – Wow! – Wow!

DUCHESS 'I speak severely to my boy –
        I **beat** him when he sneezes;
        For he can thoroughly enjoy
        The pepper when he pleases.'

CHORUS *[As before]* Wow! – Wow! – Wow!

ALICE. May I ask you a question, Your Grace?

DUCHESS. You never **stop** asking questions!

ALICE. Are you going to the palace to play croquet?

DUCHESS. I've been invited.

ALICE. So have I, and I wondered if I might go with you?

DUCHESS. The White Rabbit is to call for me. You'll have to find your **own** escort. — Little pig! Here, you may nurse it a bit, if you like.

[She throws the BABY to ALICE. The RABBIT patters on from DR and comes URC to the base of the platform.]

DUCHESS. Ah, there you are, Rabbit, and about time too!
RABBIT. *[Bowing repeatedly]* I beg pardon, Your Grace. I was delayed.
DUCHESS. You always are. *[She descends from the platform, shakes out her skirt and adjusts her headdress. The RABBIT offers his arm. He and the DUCHESS turn toward DR. ALICE comes down off the platform and the curtains close behind her on the kitchen scene.]*
ALICE Please, Mister Rabbit, I'm afraid to go to the palace alone. Mightn't I go with you?
DUCHESS. *[Gruffly]* Better not go at all!
RABBIT. The Duchess is right, my dear. You see, the Queen of Hearts is very angry with both of **us**, and if she sees **you** too — no good will come of it . . .
ALICE. But where shall I go?
DUCHESS. Attend some other party, child.

[She and the RABBIT cross down and exit DR. ALICE crosses to C with the BABY in her arms. She cradles it gently.]

ALICE. Well, at least I can look after this child. If I don't take it away, they'll surely ruin it. *[The offstage voice, which plays the BABY, begins to grunt like a pig.]* Don't grunt! That's not at all the proper way for a baby to express itself. *[More grunting and snorting. ALICE has now crossed to DL.]* If you're going to behave like a pig, my dear, I'll have nothing more to do with you. *[She sets the BABY down by the curtain. If a Halloween mask of a pig is available from a local*

*toy shop, ALICE could at this point pull back the blanket to
reveal a snout and pig's face beneath the BABY'S bonnet. A
black-gloved arm snatches it from view.]*
VOICE. *[Offstage]* Oink, oink, oink, oink! **Wheeeeee!**
ALICE. *[Staring off DL]* Eeeek, it is a pig! *[To audience]* If
  it had grown up it would have been a dreadfully ugly child.
  But it will make a rather handsome pig, I think.

Adventure 5: Cheshire cat in a tree.

*[At the UR wing, a section of leafy bough is seen.
Attached to it is the head of the CHESHIRE CAT
and a suggestion of its body and tail. The head is
a lantern, which is a duplicate of the one used in the
kitchen scene, electrified to blink on and off with its
grin separately wired.]*

CAT. *[Voice offstage]* Prrrrow . . . meowwww . . . [ALICE
  notices the CAT and goes URC to converse with it.]*
ALICE. Pussycat, they wouldn't take me with them to the
  palace. So would you tell me, please, which way I ought
  to go.
CAT. That depends on where you want to go.
ALICE. I don't care where . . .
CAT. Then it doesn't matter which way you go.
ALICE. . . . So long as I get **somewhere.**
CAT. Oh, you're sure to do that, if you only walk long enough.
ALICE. What sort of people live here?
CAT. To the east lives a Mad Hatter. To the west lives a Mad
  March Hare. Visit either you like.
ALICE. But I don't want to go among mad people.
CAT. Oh, you can't help that. We're all mad here. I'm mad.
  You're mad.
ALICE. How do you know that I'm mad?

CAT. You must be or you wouldn't be here.

ALICE. This certainly is a strange country.

CAT. Purrrfectly true. *[A few chords of soft music come under the dialogue.]* No one you meet here is quite what he seems — even to himself. That's why they call it Wonderland.

ALICE. I wish I'd never come here. It is a very frightening place.

CAT. Nobody will harm you.

ALICE. Truly?

CAT. Yes, truly. *[Music out]* Except, of course, the Queen of Hearts. She's the most bloodthirsty monarch that ever lived. Make an enemy of her and you're doomed!

ALICE. *[Downcast]* That's what I was frightened of.

CAT. Are you really going to the palace?

ALICE. *[Biting her nails]* I **may** — or I may **not.**

CAT. If you **do** go, you may see **me** there. Or you may not! *[The light in the CAT'S head fades out and it appears to vanish among the leaves. ALICE stares amazed. The CAT'S light brightens again, as it reappears.]* Bye-the-bye, what became of the baby?

ALICE. It turned into a pig.

CAT. I **thought** it would. *[Vanishes again among leaves. ALICE waits a moment to see if the CAT will reappear. As it doesn't, she turns and crosses to DLC. Then the CAT suddenly materializes once more.]* Did you say **pig** or **fig?**

ALICE. *[Turning back]* I said **pig.**

CAT. Darn!

ALICE. And I wish you wouldn't keep appearing and vanishing so suddenly!

CAT. Bye bye. *[This time the head and eyes fade out, leaving the grin clearly visible. It remains there quite a while before it too disappears.]*

ALICE. Well, I've often seen a cat without a grin, but a grin without a cat! It's most curious! *[Sound: tinkle of teacups and laughter from offstage]* I hear cups tinkling and people laughing. The March Hare must be serving rea. Perhaps as this is May, he won't be **raving** mad . . . at least not as mad as he was in March.

[She starts to exit DL. Lights black out. NOTE: The table and chairs for the following scene should be put in position during the blackout and on the lower level as close to front as possible.]

Adventure 6: The mad tea party.

[As the lights come up, the characters for the scene are seated at the table, having taken their places during the dim-out. The MARCH HARE and MAD HATTER are having tea, and the DORMOUSE is asleep between them. Although it is a long table, the three figures are crowded together behind it. There is a large tea-pot and many cups and saucers scattered about. The HARE and the HATTER talk to each other over the head of the dozing DOORMOUSE, and occasionally lean elbows on it, as though it were a cushion. They are doing exactly that, as ALICE enters DL.]

ALICE. How uncomfortable for that poor Dormouse. It's asleep, I think. *[Seeing her approach, the HARE and the HATTER begin to scream at her simultaneously.]*
BOTH. No room – no room!
ALICE. *[Calmly]* There's plenty of room! *[She crosses to the URC end of the table and seats herself.]*
HARE. I'm the March Hare. He's the Hatter. And this sleepy thing is the Dormouse. Have some wine.
ALICE. *[Looking about]* I don't see any wine.
HARE. There isn't any.
ALICE. *[Angrily]* Then it wasn't very nice of you to offer it.

HARE. It wasn't very nice of you to sit down without being invited.

ALICE. I didn't know it was **your** table.

HATTER. *[Who has been staring at ALICE]* Your hair needs cutting.

ALICE. You should learn not to make personal remarks. It's rude.

HATTER. *[Raises his eyebrows at this retort but all he says is:]* Why is a raven like a writing desk?

ALICE. I believe I can guess that.

HARE. Do you mean you think you could find out the answer to it?

ALICE. Exactly so.

HARE. Then why don't you say what you mean?

ALICE. I do. At least – at least I mean what I say – that's the same thing, you know.

HATTER. Not the same thing a bit! Why, you might just as well say that 'I see what I eat' is the same thing as 'I eat what I see!'

HARE. You might as well say that 'I like what I get' is the same thing as 'I get what I like!'

DORMOUSE. *[Talking in his sleep]* You might just as well say that 'I breathe when I sleep' is the same thing as 'I sleep when I breathe!'

HARE. It is the same with you. *[After which, the party sits silent for a long moment, thinking things over.]*

HATTER. *[Breaking the silence]* What date is it? *[He turns to ALICE. He has taken his watch from his pocket, shaking it now and then, and holding it to his ear.]*

ALICE. The fourth.

HATTER. *[With a sigh]* Two days wrong! *[Angry voice at the MARCH HARE]* I told you not to stuff butter in the gears!

HARE. *[Meekly]* It was the **best** butter. *[The MARCH HARE holds up his watch gloomily, then dips it into his cup of tea, and looks at it again, at a loss for what to say.]*

ALICE. *[Puzzled but polite]* I don't quite understand this.

HATTER. The Dormouse is asleep again. *[He pours a little tea on its nose. The DORMOUSE shakes his head impatiently.]*

DORMOUSE. *[Without opening eyes]* Of course, of course: just as you wish.

HATTER. *[Turning to ALICE]* Have you guessed the riddle yet?

ALICE. I give up. What's the answer ?

HATTER. I haven't the slightest idea.

HARE. Nor I.

ALICE. *[Wearily]* I think you might do something better with time than wasting it in asking riddles that have no answer.

HATTER. If you knew Time as well as I do, you wouldn't talk about wasting **it.** It's **him.**

ALICE. I don't know what you mean.

HATTER. *[Tossing his head contemptuously]* Of course, you don't! I dare say you never even spoke to Time!

ALICE. *[Cautiously]* Perhaps not, but I know I have to beat time when I learn music.

HATTER. Ah! That accounts for it. He won't stand beating. Now, if you'd only kept on good terms with him, he'd do almost anything you liked with the clock. For instance, suppose it were time to begin lessons. You'd only have to whisper a hint to Time, and round round goes the clock to half-past one. Time? Time? Time for dinner! Move down! *[All stand and move around to clean place settings.]*

HARE. *[In a hoarse whisper]* I only wish it was!

ALICE. *[Thoughtfully]* That would be grand, certainly, but then . . . I shouldn't be hungry.

HATTER. Not at first, perhaps, but you could keep it to half-past one as long as you liked.

ALICE. Is that the way **you** manage?

HATTER. *[Shaking his head mournfully]* Not I! We quarreled last March — just before **he** went mad, you know. *[He points*

with his teaspoon at the MARCH HARE.] It was at the great
concert given by the Queen of Hearts, and I had to sing:
[Sings]

HATTER   'Twinkle, twinkle, little bat!
            How I wonder what you're at.'

HATTER. You know the poem, perhaps?
ALICE. I've heard something like it.
HATTER. It goes on, you know, in this way —

HATTER   'Up above the world you fly,
            'Like a tea-tray in the sky.
            Twinkle, twinkle — '

DORMOUSE. *[Shakes himself and begins singing in his sleep]*
    'Twinkle, twinkle, twinkle . . . ' *[HARE and HATTER pinch
    him to make him stop.]*
HATTER. I sang that for a party once, and I'd hardly finished
    the first verse when the Queen bawled out 'He's killing time.'
    'Off with his head!' 'He's killing time.'
ALICE. *[Exclaims]* Savage!
HATTER. *[Dolefully]* Ever since, Father Time won't do a thing
    I ask! It's always four o'clock by my watch.
ALICE. *[Brightly]* Is that the reason they're so many teacups?
HATTER. *[With a sigh]* Yes, it's always teatime. We've no
    time to wash the dishes in between.
ALICE. Then you keep moving around, I suppose?
HATTER. Exactly so, as things get used up.
ALICE. But what happens when you come to the beginning
    again?
HARE. Suppose we change the subject. I vote the young lady
    tell us a story.
ALICE. *[Alarmed]* I'm afraid I don't know one.

HARE AND HATTER. Then the Dormouse shall. *[They pinch him.]* Wake up, Dormouse!

DORMOUSE. I wasn't asleep. *[He slowly opens his eyes.]*

HARE. Tell us a story!

ALICE. Yes, please do!

HATTER. And be quick about it or you'll be asleep before it's done.

DORMOUSE. *[Hurriedly]* Once upon a time there were three little sisters, and their names were Elsie, and Lacie, and Tillie; and they lived at the bottom of a well.

ALICE. What did they live on?

DORMOUSE. *[After deep thought]* They lived on maple syrup.

ALICE. *[Gently]* Very sad. They'd have been ill.

DORMOUSE. So they were — **very** ill!

HARE. *[Earnestly to ALICE]* Take some more tea.

ALICE. *[Offended]* I've had nothing yet, so I can't take more.

HATTER. You mean you can't take less. It's very easy to take more than nothing.

ALICE. Nobody asked your opinion.

HATTER. Who's making personal remarks now? *[ALICE ignores the HATTER, pours herself some tea, then turns sweetly to the DORMOUSE.]*

ALICE. Why did they live at the bottom of a well?

DORMOUSE. It was a syrup well.

ALICE. There's no such thing!

HARE AND HATTER. Sh! Sh! Sh!

DORMOUSE. *[Sulkily]* If you can't be polite, you'd better finish the story yourself.

ALICE. *[Humbly]* No, please go on!

DORMOUSE. And so, these three little sisters — they were learning to draw, you know.

ALICE. What did they draw?

DORMOUSE. Maple syrup.

HATTER. I want a clean cup. Let's all move one place. *[They do. The HATTER is the only one who gets a clean place.*

*ALICE is reluctant about moving into the HARE'S place
because of the messy plate and cups.]*

ALICE. But I don't understand. Where did they draw the syrup
from?

DORMOUSE. *[Huffily]* You can draw water out of a water
well, so I should think you could draw syrup out of a syrup
well – eh, stupid?

ALICE. But they were in the well.

DORMOUSE. Of course, they were – **well** in! *[ALICE is con-
fused, but makes no comment. The DORMOUSE is growing
sleepy and his voice slows down.]* They – were learning to
draw and they drew all manner of – things; everything that
begins with an M . . . [He snores.]*

ALICE. Why with an M?

HARE. Why **not**? *[Silence. The DORMOUSE has dozed off.
The HATTER pinches him.]*

DORMOUSE. *[Wakes with a shriek]* . . . That beings with an M,
such as mouse-traps, and the moon, and memory and muchness . . . – you know you say things are much of a muchness –
did you ever see such a thing as a drawing of a muchness?

ALICE. *[Very confused]* Really, now you ask me – I don't
think I ever have –

HATTER. Then you shouldn't talk about it!

ALICE. *[Rising in disgust]* You are **much** too rude! I shall
never take tea with you again! I should have gone to the
Queen's garden party. *[A stunned silence. The other
characters stare at ALICE in consternation.]*

HARE. *[A hushed voice]* Do you mean to say you were invited to play croquet?

ALICE. I was.

HATTER. *[Equally aghast]* And you didn't **go**?

ALICE. *[Sedately]* I haven't yet. *[HARE and HATTER leap
up, seize her by the arms.]*

HARE AND HATTER. *[Shouting]* Then you must go! Now!
You must go at once! Don't wait another minute! The Queen's
waiting.

DORMOUSE. *[Shrilly]* Yes, go! *[Chase music begins and continues to close of scene.]*

HARE. Do you realize what could happen to us?

HATTER. If you've antagonized Her Majesty, heads will roll!

DORMOUSE. Heads will roll!

ALICE. Oh dear, if I must go, I must. I want to keep my head. And how do I find the palace? *[They escort her from the table and run her off in the direction of DR.]*

HARE. Go up the hill till you come to a big mulberry bush.

DORMOUSE. *[Circling ALICE]* Then you go round the mulberry bush.

HATTER. You'll see the palace and the royal croquet ground.

HARE. You can't possibly miss it. Go on, go on! Hurry!! *[The HARE, HATTER and DORMOUSE stand C, as they wave goodbye to ALICE, urging her onward.]*

ALL. Hurry, or heads will roll! You mustn't be late!

ALICE. *[Calling ahead]* I'm hurrying as fast as ever I can. Please, dear Queen, don't be angry — oh, my poor head! I can't lose my head.

[CURTAIN]

ALICE IN WONDERLAND

ACT II

Adventure 7: The royal croquet ground.

AT RISE OF CURTAIN: The lights come up on the tableau stage. The curtains have parted to reveal a garden. C stage is a large rose tree with white roses on it, and three playing-card GARDENERS with brushes and buckets are at work painting the blossoms red. ALICE enters from R at stage level and stands observing the action.

2 OF SPADES. Look out now, Five. Don't go splashing paint over me like that.

5 OF SPADES. I couldn't help it. Seven jogged my elbow.

7 OF SPADES. That's right, Five. Always lay the blame on others.

5 OF SPADES. You'd better not talk. I heard the Queen say you should be beheaded.

2 OF SPADES. What for?

7 OF SPADES. That's none of your business.

5 OF SPADES. Yes, it is his business, and I'll tell him. It was for bringing the cook tulip bulbs instead of onions.

7 OF SPADES. Well, of all the unjust things! *[He catches sight of ALICE. They turn toward her and bow.]*

2 OF SPADES. Who is she?

ALICE. *[Making a curtsy]* Would you tell me, please, why you're painting those roses? *[FIVE and SEVEN look at TWO, waiting for him to answer.]*

2 OF SPADES. Why, the fact is, you see, Miss, this here ought to have been a **red** rose tree and we planted a white one by mistake, and if the Queen was to find it out, we'd all have our heads cut off, you know. *[A blare of trumpets is heard offstage L.]*

5 OF SPADES. *[Pointing off L]* The Queen! The Queen! *[The three GARDENERS leave upper platform, run DRC and fall flat on their faces in panic. ALICE crossed UR to watch the royal entrance. Another trumpet is heard.]*

VOICES. *[Offstage]* Make way for her Royal Majesty! Gangway for the Queen of Hearts!

[Enter the procession. First, PAGES and HERALDS with trumpets, all wearing playing card sign boards. Then, comes the QUEEN OF HEARTS, imperious and forbidding; followed by the KING OF HEARTS, who is a dunce and the KNAVE OF HEARTS, a simpering fop. Stage space permitting, there should be two SOLDIERS with spears, flanking the EXECUTIONER with his axe. The QUEEN OF HEARTS holds up her hand to halt the parade. She addresses herself to ALICE pointing a disdainful finger.]

QUEEN OF HEARTS. Who is **this**? What is your name, child?

ALICE. *[Making a curtsy]* My name is Alice. Your Majesty, we met this morning.

QUEEN OF HEARTS. Alice, to be sure. *[Pointing to the prostrate GARDENERS]* And who are **these**?

ALICE. *[A little taken aback at her own courage]* How should I know, Your Majesty? This is **your** croquet garden.

QUEEN OF HEARTS. *[Glaring furiously]* Off with her head! Off with her head, I say! *[The SOLDIERS advance.]*

KING OF HEARTS. *[Intervening]* Consider, my dear. She is only a child.

QUEEN OF HEARTS. I forgive her on the grounds of youth.
[To the KNAVE] Turn them over!

KNAVE. *[Timorously]* Yes, auntie — I mean, **yes,** Your Royal
Majesty! *[The KNAVE goes URC and with a dainty foot
turns the three GARDENERS over, as if they were turtles.
They lie on their backs palpitating with fear.]*

QUEEN OF HEARTS. Get them on their feet. The miserable
wretches! *[The GARDENERS rise and begin bowing
frantically.]* Stop that ridiculous bowing. You make
me giddy. *[Points to rose tree]* What have you been doing
here?

2 OF SPADES. May it please Your Majesty, we were trying —

QUEEN OF HEARTS. Off with their heads!

5 OF SPADES. Spare us, Majesty! Have mercy!

QUEEN OF HEARTS. Take them away!

*[Playing card SOLDIERS hustle the GARDENERS off R.
The EXECUTIONER strides after them with axe on
shoulder. The QUEEN turns graciously to ALICE, as
though nothing unusual had occurred.]*

QUEEN OF HEARTS. Do you play croquet, my dear?

ALICE. *[Trembling]* Yes, Your Majesty.

QUEEN OF HEARTS. Come along then.

*[The WHITE RABBIT patters in from L and hands the
QUEEN and ALICE prop flamingos. QUEEN holds hers
upside down wielding it like a mallet.]*

QUEEN OF HEARTS. At my court, we use flamingos for
mallets. So amusing, don't you agree?

*[Exit the QUEEN OF HEARTS and her entourage. ALICE
lingers for a word with the RABBIT. Curtains close on
tableau stage.]*

ALICE. Is she really going to chop off their heads?
RABBIT. Well, yes. *[Timid]* Fine day, isn't it.
ALICE. Perhaps, but where's the Duchess?
RABBIT. *[Whisper]* Shhhh! She's going to be executed!
ALICE. Good gracious! What for?
RABBIT. She punched the Queen of Hearts in the nose. *[ALICE laughs out loud.]* Quiet, the Queen will hear you! You see, the Duchess was late to the party, and the Queen was furious.
QUEEN OF HEARTS. *[Offstage]* Off with her head! *[Screams]*
ALICE. That's terrible!
QUEEN OF HEARTS. *[Off]* Off with his head! *[Screams]*
ALICE. Rabbit, tell me something, please . . .
QUEEN OF HEARTS. *[Off]* Off with **everyone's** head! *[Screams and running offstage]*
ALICE. I must go home. Tell me how.
RABBIT. What a temper. Home? Home? Just ask the Queen. She'll know.
ALICE. I don't dare!

[Enter DUCHESS from DL.]

ALICE. Your Majesty!
RABBIT. Ask the Duchess. I think she knows. But I don't think she'll tell you. She's too upset about losing her head.
QUEEN OF HEARTS. *[Calling off]* Where is that Rabbit? Rabbit, I want **you!**
RABBIT. *[Calling off]* Coming! Coming!

[Hasty exit R]

DUCHESS. *[Exuding social charm]* You can't think how glad I am to see you again, you dear old thing. *[ALICE doesn't answer. She's astounded.]* You're thinking about something, my dear, and that makes you forget to talk. I can't tell you just what the moral of that is, but I shall remember it in a bit.

ALICE. The Queen wants to chop off your head. What's the
  moral of that?

DUCHESS. Tut, tut, child! **Everything's** got a moral if you can
  find it. How are you getting on? How do you like the Queen?

ALICE. Not at all. She's so fond of beheading people, the wonder
  is, that there's any one left alive!

DUCHESS. You didn't enjoy the croquet?

ALICE. Not the way they play it here.

DUCHESS. What do you think of **me**, my dear?

ALICE. Well, when I'm a Duchess, I won't have any pepper in
  my kitchen **at all**. Maybe it's pepper that makes people hot-
  tempered — and vinegar that makes them sour — and sugar
  cookies that make children sweet-tempered. *[The DUCHESS
  rests her chin on ALICE'S shoulder and suddenly weeps.]*

DUCHESS. Oh, I'm frightened! I've never lost my head before.
  [She sniffles.] And the moral of this is — 'love makes the
  world go round.'

ALICE. *[Comforting her]* There, there, how fond you are of
  finding morals in things!

DUCHESS. *[Affectionate]* You're wondering why I don't put
  my arm round your waist. The reason is I'm doubtful about
  the temper of your flamingo . . . Shall I try the experiment?

ALICE. He might bite.

DUCHESS. Very true. *[Intimate]* Flamingoes and mustard both
  bite. And the moral of that is — 'birds of a feather flock
  together.'

ALICE. Only mustard isn't a bird.

DUCHESS. *[Cheering up]* Right, as usual. What a clear way
  you have of putting things!

ALICE. Mustard is a mineral, I **think**.

DUCHESS. Of course, it is. *[Almost bragging]* There's a large
  mustard-mine near here. And the moral of that is — 'The
  more there is of mine, the less there is of yours.'

ALICE. I'd understand that better if I had it written down.

DUCHESS. *[Pleased with herself]* That's nothing to what I
  could say!

[The QUEEN enters.]

DUCHESS. *[Seeing the QUEEN she breaks off in midsentence. Weakly]* A fine day, Your Majesty. *[Bows]*
QUEEN OF HEARTS. *[Shouting and stamping her feet]* I give you fair warning: you must get ready for your execution, or I'll chop off your head!

[The DUCHESS scurries out DL, weeping. The QUEEN turns to ALICE with a smile.]

QUEEN OF HEARTS. Have you seen the Mock Turtle yet?
ALICE. I don't even know what a Mock Turtle is.
QUEEN OF HEARTS. It's the thing Mock Turtle soup is made from. *[Taking ALICE'S flamingo]* Go along, and he'll tell you his story . . . *[Calls to offstage R]* Gryphon! *[No answer]* Gryphon!!

[The GRYPHON slouches on from DR.]

ALICE. Is that a Mock Turtle?
QUEEN OF HEARTS. No, foolish girl. That's a Gryphon.
GRYPHON. *[Growls]* Grrr-rrrr!
QUEEN OF HEARTS. Stir your stumps, you lazy thing! And take this young lady to the Mock Turtle. I must go see to the executions.

[She marches off R. Lights fade, except for a pinspot which picks out ALICE and the GRYPHON at DL.]

GRYPHON. *[A slight cockney accent]* You heard what Her Bloomin' Majesty said! Come on, now! Don't dilly-dally.

[Exits DL]

ALICE. Right. I've never been so glad to leave a place in all my life.

[She follows the GRYPHON out DL. Spotlight blacks out.]

Adventure 8: Mock Turtle on a beach.

[As lights come up again, ALICE and the GRYPHON re-enter from DL. The upstage C curtains have been opened to reveal the MOCK TURTLE, seated on a ledge by the seaside, sighing and weeping as if his heart were about to break. ALICE and GRYPHON pause DLC.]

ALICE. Why is he crying, poor fellow?
GRYPHON. It's all in his head. Come on! *[They go to the platform where the TURTLE is sitting.]* This 'ere young lady, she wants for to know your 'istory, she do.
TURTLE. *[A deep hollow voice]* I'll tell her. Sit down and don't speak a word till I've finished. *[They sit down at the base of the platform. The TURTLE rises and clears his throat.]* Once . . . I was a **real** turtle. *[Sighs]* When we were little, we went to school in the sea. The master was an old turtle — we used to call him Tortoise.
ALICE. Why did you call him Tortoise if he wasn't one?
TURTLE. We called him Tortoise because he was a teacher and he taught us. *[With asperity]* Really you **are** very dull!
GRYPHON. You ought to be ashymed of yourself for asking such a simple question.
TURTLE. Yes, we went to school in the sea, though you mayn't believe it —
ALICE. I never said I didn't —
TURTLE. You did!
GRYPHON. *[Before ALICE can talk]* Hold your tongue!
TURTLE. We had the best of educations. In fact, we went to school every day.

ALICE. I've been to day school too. You needn't be so proud as all that.

TURTLE. *[A little anxiously]* With extras?

ALICE. Yes, French and Music.

TURTLE. And Washing?

ALICE. *[Indignant]* Certainly not!

TURTLE. Ah! Then yours wasn't a really good school. Now at **ours** they had — French, Music **and Washing**, extra.

ALICE. You couldn't have needed it much, living at the bottom of the sea.

TURTLE. *[Sadly]* I couldn't afford to learn it. I only took the regular course.

ALICE. What was that?

TURTLE. Reeling and Writhing, of course, to begin with. And then the different branches of Arithmetic — Ambition, Distraction, Uglification and Derision.

ALICE. I never heard of Uglification.

GRYPHON. *[Raising paws in horror]* Never heard of Uglification? You know what to beautify is, I suppose.

ALICE. It means to make anything — prettier.

GRYPHON. Well, then, if you don't know what to uglify is, you **are** a simpleton.

ALICE. *[Hastily]* And how many hours a day did you do lessons?

TURTLE. Ten hours the first day, nine the next, and so on.

ALICE. What a curious plan!

GRYPHON. That's the reason they are called lessons. Because they lessen from day to day.

ALICE. *[Thoughtfully]* Then the eleventh day must have been a holiday.

TURTLE. Of course, it was.

ALICE. But how did you manage on the twelfth?

GRYPHON. *[Decisively]* That's enough about lessons. Tell her something about the games. *[The MOCK TURTLE is momentarily overcome with weeping, but the GRYPHON slaps him on the back and he recovers.]*

TURTLE. Thank you. *[To ALICE]* You may not have lived
   much under the sea.
ALICE. I haven't.
TURTLE. And perhaps you were never introduced to a Lobster.
ALICE. I once tasted — *[Thinks better of it]* No, never!
TURTLE. So you have no idea what a delightful thing a Lobster
   Quardrille is.
ALICE. A Quadrille? Isn't that a dance?
TURTLE. Would you like to see a little of it?
ALICE. Very much.
TURTLE. *[To GRYPHON]* Come, let's dance the Lobster Quadrille.
   It can be managed without lobsters, don't you know.
ALICE. Will the Queen allow it?
TURTLE. We won't tell her.
GRYPHON. You sing! I forgot the words. *[The TURTLE sings
   solemnly, as he and the GRYPHON mime a grotesque minuet.
   When they come to the refrain 'Will you, won't you?' the
   GRYPHON grabs ALICE and whirls her about.]*

MOCK
TURTLE   'Will you walk a little faster!' said a whiting to
                  a snail.
             'There's a porpoise close behind us, and he's treading
                  on my tail . . .
             See how eagerly the lobsters and the turtles all
                  advance!
             They are waiting on the shingle — will you come and
                  join the dance?
             Will you, won't you, will you, won't you, will you
                  join the dance?
             Will you, won't you, will you, won't you, won't
                  you join the dance?'

             'You can really have no notion how delightful
                  it will be
             When they take us up and throw us, with the lobsters
                  out to sea!'

The further off from England the nearer 'tis to
France,
Then turn not pale, beloved snail, but come and join
the dance.
Would not, could not, would not, could not, would
not join the dance?
Would not, could not, would not, could not, could
not join the dance.

ALICE. Thank you! It's a very interesting dance. And I like
that funny part about the whiting.
GHYPHON. Do you know why it's called a whiting?
ALICE. No.
GRYPHON. *[Solemnly]* It polishes our boots.
ALICE. The whiting polishes your boots?
GRYPHON. What are **your** shoes done with?
ALICE. With blacking, I believe . . .
GRYPHON. *[Impressively]* Boots and shoes under the sea are
done with whiting. Now you know. *[ALICE claps her
hands with pleasure at the joke.]*
ALICE. And what are they made of?
GRYPHON. Soles and eels, of course. *[She claps again.]* Any
shrimp could have told you that.
ALICE. If I'd been the whiting in the song, I'd have told the
porpoise, 'Keep back, please, we don't want you with us.'
TURTLE. *[Interrupting]* No wise fish would go anywhere without
a porpoise.
ALICE. *[Mock serious]* Wouldn't it really?
TURTLE. Of course not. If a fish came to me and told me he
was going on a journey, I'd say, 'With what porpoise?'
GRYPHON. Shall we dance again? Or would you like the Mock
Turtle to sing you a song?
ALICE. Oh, a **song**, please!
GRYPHON. *[Irked]* No accounting for tastes. Sing her Turtle
Soup, will you, old fellow? *[For his song, the MOCK TURTLE
comes DC. ALICE and GRYPHON follow. Upstage
curtains close.]*

TURTLE   'Beautiful Soup so rich and green,
            Waiting in a hot tureen!
            Who for such dainties would not stoop?
            Soup of the evening, beautiful soup!

            Soup of the evening, beautiful soup!
            Beau-ootiful soo-oop!
            Beau-ootiful-soo-oop!
            Soo-oop of the e-e-e-evening,
            Beautiful, beautiful soup!

*[The WHITE RABBIT and two playing card SOLDIERS
march in from L and confront ALICE.]*

RABBIT. You are under arrest!
ALICE. *[Horrified]* I am???
RABBIT. Anything you say may be used against you.
ALICE. What am I arrested for?
RABBIT. The Knave of Hearts stole some tarts. You are
    suspected of being a necessity after the fact.
ALICE. That's ridiculous! I never met the Knave of Hearts.
RABBIT. Come along quietly. Or you shall be beheaded. March!

*[The SOLDIERS put chains on ALICE'S wrists and lead
her off as the lights black out.]*

Adventure 9: Who stole the tarts?

[In the darkness, we can hear the WHITE RABBIT pro-claim: 'Hear ye! Hear ye! The trial's beginning! The trial's beginning!' Fanfare of trumpets. Lights up. The KING and QUEEN OF HEARTS are seated on thrones under a canopy on the tableau stage. As many other WONDERLAND CREATURES as can be crowded on-stage are present as audience and jury. The WHITE RABBIT in heraldic tabard and cape takes his place behind a table on which are a platter of tarts, the evidence, marked with a sign : 'Exhibit A.' ALICE and the KNAVE OF HEARTS, in chains and watched by guards are DR. A chair for WITNESSES is DL. Hubbub of voices gradually subsides.]

ALICE. I wish they'd get this absurd trial over with and pass round the tarts. They look delicious.

ALL. Shush! Silence in court!

ALICE. I wish to state that I am totally innocent of the charges brought against me.

QUEEN OF HEARTS. Off with her head, I say!

RABBIT. Silence in court!

KING OF HEARTS. *[Adjusting his spectacles]* Herald, read the accusation!

RABBIT. *[Unrolling a scroll]*
'The Queen of Hearts, she made some tarts,
    All on a summer day:
The Knave of Hearts, he stole those tarts
    And took them quite away!'

ALICE. I had nothing to do with it.

KING OF HEARTS. Consider your verdict.

RABBIT. Not yet, not yet. There's a great deal to come before that.

KING OF HEARTS. Then call the first witness.

45

RABBIT. First witness! Mad Hatter! Mad Hatter!

[MAD HATTER hurries in from DR and goes to witness box ULC. He holds a teacup in one hand and a piece of bread and butter in the other.]

QUEEN OF HEARTS. Hurry up! We haven't got all day!

HATTER. I **beg** your pardon, Your Majesty!

QUEEN OF HEARTS. It isn't respectable to beg.

HATTER. I mean, I'm sorry for bringing these in. But I hadn't quite finished my tea.

QUEEN OF HEARTS. When did you begin?

HATTER. Fourteenth of March, I think it was.

HARE. *[Comes forward and speaks up]* It was the fifteenth.

QUEEN OF HEARTS. Jury, write that down. *[Muttering as JURY jots notes on notepads.]*

RABBIT. Silence in court!

QUEEN OF HEARTS. *[To HATTER]* Witness, take off your hat!

HATTER. It isn't mine. *[In a quavering voice]* I'm a poor man, Your Majesty, and I hadn't but just begun my tea, and what with the bread and butter getting so expensive and the twinkling of the tea-tray —

KING OF HEARTS. The twinkling of **what?**

HATTER. It began with the tea.

KING OF HEARTS. Of course, twinkling begins with a T. Do you take me for a dunce? If that's all you know, you may stand down.

HATTER. I can't go any lower. I'm on the floor as it is.

KING OF HEARTS. Then you may sit down.

HATTER. I'd rather go home and finish my tea.

KING OF HEARTS. You may go!

HATTER. *[Shaking a finger at ALICE]* But mark my words, she's a very peculiar girl. Just the kind to go stealing other people's tarts.

[The HATTER runs off L, followed by the HARE.]

QUEEN OF HEARTS. *[Hissing]* Suspicious! Very suspicious!
  She said at home she often helped herself to tarts without
  permission. I think the girl should be beheaded on principle.
KING OF HEARTS. *[To JURY]* Consider your verdict.
RABBIT. There's more evidence to come, Your Majesty. I've
  just been handed this paper. It's a set of verses.
QUEEN OF HEARTS. Suspicious!
KING OF HEARTS. Are they in handwriting of either prisoner.
KNAVE. Not in mine!
ALICE. Not in mine!
RABBIT. Shall I read it anyway, Your Majesty?
KING OF HEARTS. *[Gravely]* Begin at the beginning and go
  on till you come to the end; then stop!
RABBIT. *[Reads]*
  'They told me you had been to her,
      And mentioned me to him;
  She gave me a good character,
      But said I could not swim.'
KING OF HEARTS. *[Rubbing his hands]* That's the most im-
  portant piece of evidence we've heard! Now let the jury
  proceed.
ALICE. *[Crossing DC]* If any of the jury can explain it, I'll give
  him sixpence. I don't believe there's an atom of meaning in it!
JURY. *[Softly and simultaneously, jotting notes]* She – doesn't –
  be – lieve – there's an a – tom of mean – ing in it . . .
KING OF HEARTS. *[He is examining the paper, handed him by
  the RABBIT, through a large magnifying glass.]* I do seem to
  see some meaning – 'I said I could not **swim** – ' You **can't**
  swim, can you?
KNAVE. *[Forlornly]* Do I look like I could?
KING OF HEARTS. *[To JURY]* You heard him confess! Consider your verdict.
QUEEN OF HEARTS. No, no. Sentence first, verdict later.

ALICE. That's illegal!

QUEEN OF HEARTS. Hold your tongue. *[Everyone in the assembly holds their tongues.]* Alice, I said hold your tongue.

ALICE. I won't. *[The assembly advances on ALICE.]*

QUEEN OF HEARTS. I said hold your tongue. Now!

ALICE. I won't do it.

QUEEN OF HEARTS. *[Screams]* Off with her head.

ALL. Off with her head.

QUEEN OF HEARTS. Off with her head.

ALL. Off with her head.

ALICE. Stop! Stop! I haven't done anything. I just want to go home.

QUEEN OF HEARTS. Off with her head.

ALL. Off with her head.

ALICE. Rabbit, help me! Duchess, help!

RABBIT. She lost her head.

ALICE. Stop! *[Climbing atop the witness box]* You can't do this to me. I'm not afraid. Do you hear? *[Everyone abruptly silent]* You're not real! You're just a pack of cards! *[Wavering]* Oh, no! Please —

[The crowd attacks. Flashing lightning effects. Pinwheel spots. An avalanche of cards flutters down from above in a colored snowstorm. ALICE fights off the crowd as music rises to a crescendo. She runs offstage as trumpets blare and drums roll and rumble like thunder.]

[CURTAIN]

ALICE IN WONDERLAND

ACT III

Adventure 10: The Red Queen.

AT RISE OF CURTAIN: As the lights come up, ALICE is in headlong flight, in front of a chessboard backdrop, as though pursued by the pack of playing cards. The spots and pinwheels are still gyrating in a kaleidoscopic effect. She runs from DL to DR, makes a figure eight tour of the stage and winds up at downstage C, running in place, without moving forward. A wind effect is heard. Presently, the RED QUEEN runs into view from R, and as sound and light effects diminish, the two characters find themselves face to face at DC. They stop their exertions to catch their breath.

RED QUEEN. Where do you come from and where are you going? Look up, speak nicely, and don't twiddle your fingers.

ALICE. *[Breathless]* I'm sorry. You see I've lost my way.

RED QUEEN. I don't know what you mean by **your** way. I'm the Red Queen. All the ways about here belong to **me** — but why did you come here at all?

ALICE. I only wanted to see what your garden was like, Your Majesty.

RED QUEEN. *[She pats ALICE on the head.]* When you say 'garden' — **I've** seen gardens, compared with which this would be a wilderness.

ALICE. — And I thought I'd try to find my way to the top of that hill.

RED QUEEN. When you say 'hill' – I could show you hills, in comparison with which you'd call that a valley.

ALICE. No, I shouldn't, a hill can't be a valley, you know. That would be nonsense –

RED QUEEN. I've heard nonsense, compared with which that would be as sensible as a dictionary! *[ALICE curtsies out of politeness.]*

ALICE. *[Surveying the view]* This must be Looking-Glass Land. It's marked out just like a large chessboard. A huge game of chess that's being played – all over the world – if this is the world at all. Wait! I remember! If I can cross the chessboard I'll become a Queen, and if I become a Queen, I can go home! *[She glances at the QUEEN, who smiles back agreeably.]*

RED QUEEN. That's easily managed. When you get to the Eighth Square you'll be a Queen. Come along! *[They begin to run hand in hand. Wind effect surges offstage, then fades to background. The RED QUEEN is ahead of ALICE who can scarcely keep up.]* Faster! Faster! Don't try to talk! *[ALICE falls back a little.]* Faster! Faster!

ALICE. *[Regaining her breath]* It's cold! Are we nearly there?

RED QUEEN. Nearly there! Why, we passed it ten minutes ago! *[They run again in silence.]* Now! Faster! Faster! *[ALICE falls behind again, and sinks to ground. The wind dies away. The QUEEN sits beside ALICE and addresses her kindly.]* You may rest a little now, my dear.

ALICE. *[Shivering]* We've been in this same place the whole time!

RED QUEEN. Of course we have.

ALICE. In our country, you'd generally get to somewhere else – if you ran very fast for a long time.

RED QUEEN. Here, you see, it takes all the running you can do to keep in the same place. If you want to get somewhere else, you must run at least as twice as fast as that.

ALICE. *[Sadly]* How dreadful! I'll never get home.

RED QUEEN. *[Hugging ALICE warmly]* Remember, this is
Looking Glass Land. If you hold the word **evil** up to a mirror,
it's simply **live** spelled backwards.
ALICE. I guess you're right.
RED QUEEN. So cheer up. Take another example. Look at this
poetry book. *[Removes small book from pocket and gives it
to ALICE, who examines it curiously.]*
ALICE. Why, it's backwards!
RED QUEEN. Of course, you've come through the looking
glass. *[The QUEEN has a hand mirror attached by a cord to
her belt. She extends the mirror and ALICE holds up the
book close to the glass.]*
ALICE. It's called 'Jabberwocky.' *[Reading]*
'Twas brilling, and the slithy toves
Did grye and gimble in the wabe;
All mimsy were the borogoves,
And the mome raths outgrabe.

'Beware the Jabberwock, my son!
The jaws that bite, the claws that catch!
Beware the Jubjub bird, and shun
The frumious Bandersnatch!'

And as in uffish thought he stood,
The Jabberwock, with eyes of flame,
Came whiffling through the tulgey wood,
And burbled as it came!

One, two! One, two! And through and through
The vorpal blade went snicker-snack!
He left it dead, and with its head
He went galumphing back.

It doesn't make sense.

RED QUEEN. It does to me. Perhaps we should run a bit and clear away the cobwebs.

ALICE. I rather not try to run any more, please. I'm so hot and thirsty.

RED QUEEN. *[Takes a large biscuit out of her pocket.]* Have a dry biscuit? *[ALICE tests the cracker but finds it stonelike. She coughs and puts it in her pocket.]* While you're refreshing yourself, I'll just take the measurements. *[She marches to a point downstage R, and begins to measure distances on the ground with a tape measure, taking sidesteps left to right, and the end of each square foot bouncing and bending her knees, and making pantomime gestures, as though placing pegs at intervals.]* At the end of two yards . . . *[She dodges two steps L. Bounces up and down.]* I shall give you your directions. Have another biscuit?

ALICE. No, thank you, one's **quite** enough.

RED QUEEN. Thirst quenched, I hope? *[Paces three steps . . .]* I shall pace them before I forget them. **Three!** . . . **Four!** . . . And I must say goodbye at the end of **Five!** *[She is back at her starting point, walking about in tiny squares.]* Here's how to cross the chessboard. Listen. A pawn goes two squares in it's first move, you know. *[Jumping rapidly from one point to another to illustrate]* So you go **very** quickly through the Third Square . . . and you'll find yourself in the Fourth Square in no time . . . but **that** square belongs to **Tweedledum** and **Tweedledee** . . . the Fifth is mostly water . . . and the Sixth belongs to **Humpty Dumpty** . . . You'll have to deal with him however you can — Have you nothing to say?

ALICE. I . . . I . . . didn't know I had to say anything just then.

RED QUEEN. The Seventh Square is all forest . . . and in the Eighth Square we'll be Queens together. It's all feasting and fun! *[She turns to ALICE, who rises and curtsies.]* Off we go! *[She faces R and starts running in place.]*

ALICE. She **can** run very fast!

RED QUEEN. Good-bye, my little dear!

*[She exits DR. ALICE waves good-bye. Then she herself
exits DL. The lights dim down, but only part way. To
the faint sound of martial music we see the shadowy
figures of the KING and QUEEN OF HEARTS, the
HEADSMAN with his glittering blade, and a file of
SOLDIERS in stealthy pursuit of the fugitive ALICE.
They cross from DR to DL and exit, as the lights
black out completely.]*

Adventure 11: Tweedledum and Tweedledee.

*[Lights pinspot two plump figures DLC. They are standing
motionless, facing front, each with an arm about the other's
neck. One has 'DUM' on his collar, the other has 'DEE.'
Intrigued, ALICE walks about them in a circle, examining
them from all sides. She is startled when one of them
speaks.]*

TWEEDLEDUM. If you think we're statues you ought to pay,
you know. Statues aren't made to be looked at for nothing
nohow!
TWEEDLEDEE. On the other hand, if you think we're alive
you ought to speak.
ALICE. I'm very sorry.
TWEEDLEDUM. I know what you're thinking about, but it
isn't so, nohow.
TWEEDLEDEE. Contrariwise. If it was so, it might be; and if
it were so, it would be, but as it isn't, it ain't. That's logic.
ALICE. I was thinking which is the best way across the chess-
board. It's getting dark. Would you tell me, please? *[TWEEDLE-
DUM and TWEEDLEDEE look at each other and grin.]*
TWEEDLEDEE. You like poetry?

ALICE. **Some** poetry . . .

TWEEDLEDEE. What shall we repeat to her?

TWEEDLEDUM. *[Hugging his brother]* 'The Walrus and the
Carpenter.' That's the longest.

ALICE. If it's very long, would you tell me, first which road
to take . . .

TWEEDLEDEE. Sit down and listen! *[If desired, extras in
costumes for WALRUS, CARPENTER and OYSTERS can
pantomine the poem's action in front of ALICE. TWEEDLE-
DUM and TWEEDLEDEE have glided to DC, still with their
arms around each other's necks, ready to recite. ALICE sits
crosslegged on the ground DR, prepared to listen.]*

> 'The Walrus and the Carpenter
>   Were walking on the strand.
> They wept like anything to see
>   Such quantities of sand:
> 'If this were only cleared away,'
>   They said, 'it would be grand!'

[To ALICE] Sit down!

TWEEDLEDUM.

> 'O Oysters, come and walk with us!'
>   The Walrus did beseech.
> 'A pleasant walk, a pleasant talk,
>   Along the briny beach:
> We cannot do with more than four,
>   To give a hand to each.'

[To ALICE] Sit down!

TWEEDLEDEE.

> Then four young Oysters hurried up,
>   All eager for the treat:
> Their coats were brushed, their faces
>   washed,
>   Their shoes were clean and neat —
> And this was odd, because, you know,
>   They hadn't any feet.

[To ALICE] Sit down!

TWEEDLEDUM.

> Four other Oysters followed them,
>> And yet another four:
> And thick and fast they came at last,
>> And more, and more, and more —
> All hopping through the frothy waves,
>> And scrambling to the shore.

[To ALICE] Sit down!

TWEEDLEDEE.

> The Walrus and the Carpenter
>> Walked on a mile or so,
> And then they rested on a rock
>> Conveniently low:
> And all the little Oysters stood
>> And waited in a row.

[To ALICE] Sit down!

TWEEDLEDUM.

> 'The time has come,' the Walrus said,
>> 'To talk of many things:
> Of shoes — and ships — and sealing wax —
>> Of cabbages — and kings —
> Any why the sea is boiling hot —
>> And whether pigs have wings.'

[To ALICE] Sit down!

TWEEDLEDEE.

> 'A loaf of bread,' the Walrus said,
>> 'Is what we chiefly need:
> Pepper and vinegar besides
>> Are very good indeed—
> Now, if you're ready, Oysters dear,
>> We can begin to feed.'

[To ALICE] Sit down.

TWEEDLEDUM.

> 'But not on us!' the Oysters cried,
>> Turning a little blue.

     'After such kindness that would be
      A dismal thing to do!'
     'The night is fine,' the Walrus said.
      'Do you admire the view?'
  [To ALICE] Sit down.
TWEEDLEDEE.

     'It seems a shame,' the Walrus said,
      To play them such a trick.
     After we've brought them out so far,
      And made them trot so quick!'
     The Carpenter said nothing but
      'The butter's spread too thick!'
  [To ALICE] Sit down!
TWEEDLEDUM.

     'I weep for you,' the Walrus said:
      'I deeply sympathize.'
     With sobs and tears he sorted out
      Those of the largest size,
     Holding his pocket-handkerchief
      Before his streaming eyes.
  [To ALICE] One more verse!
TWEEDLEDUM AND TWEEDLEDEE. *[In unison]*

     'O Oysters,' said the Carpenter,
      'You've had a pleasant run!
     Shall we be trotting home again?'
      But answer came there none —
     And this was scarcely odd, because
      They'd eaten every one.'

 [They bow.]

ALICE. *[Applauds politely]* I like the Walrus best, because he was a **little** sorry for the poor oysters.

TWEEDLEDEE. He ate more than the Carpenter, though. He held his handkerchief in front, so the Carpenter couldn't count how many he took.

ALICE. Well, that was a very unpleasant tale. Now please, please tell me the way to the White Queen! I'm lost and I think it's going to rain. *[The general lighting has begun to dim. TWEEDLEDEE crosses to DR and picks up an enormous umbrella, which is on the floor behind the proscenium wing. He opens the umbrella and his brother joins him under its shelter.]*
BOTH. Don't get wet!

[The TWEEDLE brothers exit R.]

ALICE. Selfish things! I'm lost and I do so need help! Somebody please help.

Adventure 12: The White Queen.

[Lights flash on and off rapidly. Thunder is heard, and a wind effect. ALICE has followed to DRC position, as the TWEEDLE brothers exit. Now a white shawl is thrown onstage, which covers ALICE'S head and face. She shakes herself free of it, and examines the shawl in surprise.

ALICE. Somebody's shawl has been blown off.

[The WHITE QUEEN is now blown into view from off R. She whirls about wildly, frightened and helpless with arms outstretched, and eyes ablaze. She winds up at C stage in a grotesquely twisted attitude.]

WHITE QUEEN. *[Muttering]* Bread-and-butter, bread-and-butter, bread-and-butter.
ALICE. *[Facing her timidly]* Am I addressing the White Queen?
WHITE QUEEN. I'd call it 'undressing.'

ALICE. *[Commenting on the QUEEN'S disheveled costume]*
May I put your shawl straight for you?

WHITE QUEEN. *[Forlornly]* It's out of temper, I think. I've
pinned it here and I've pinned it there, but there's no pleasing
it!

ALICE. It can't go straight, you know, if you pin it all on one
side. Dear me, what a state your hair is in.

WHITE QUEEN. The brush got entangled in it and I lost the
comb yesterday. *[ALICE untangles the brush from the
QUEEN'S wig and rearranges a few hairpins.]*

ALICE. You look rather better now. But really you should
have a lady's maid.

WHITE QUEEN. You're very sweet. I'll hire **you** with pleasure!
Tuppence a week and jam every other day.

ALICE. I don't want you to hire **me** — and I don't much care
for jam. But if you would show me the road across the chessboard?

WHITE QUEEN. It's very good jam.

ALICE. Well, I don't want any today.

WHITE QUEEN. You couldn't have it if you **did**. The rule is
jam tomorrow and jam yesterday but never jam **today**.

ALICE. It must come sometimes to 'Jam today.'

WHITE QUEEN. No it can't! It's jam every **other** day. Today
isn't any other day, you know.

ALICE. I don't understand.

WHITE QUEEN. That's the effect of living backwards, it makes
one a little giddy.

ALICE. I never heard of living backwards.

WHITE QUEEN. There is one great advantage. One's memory
works both ways.

ALICE. **Mine** only works one way. I can't remember things
before they happen.

WHITE QUEEN. It's a poor memory that only works backwards.

ALICE. What sort of things do **you** remember best?

WHITE QUEEN. *[Carelessly]* Oh, things that happened the week
after next. For instance now *[She sticks a piece of adhesive
tape to her forefinger.]* there's the King's Messenger. He's in
prison now, being punished: and the trial doesn't even begin
till next Wednesday: and of course the crime comes last of
all.

ALICE. Suppose he never commits the crime?

WHITE QUEEN. That would be all the better, wouldn't it? *[She
is now winding gauze bandage around the finger.]*

ALICE. Of course, it would be all the better, but it wouldn't
be all the better his being punished.

WHITE QUEEN. You're wrong **there**, at any rate! Were **you**
ever punished?

ALICE. Only for faults.

WHITE QUEEN. *[Triumphantly]* And you were all the better for
it, I know! − ow − ow! *[Her voice has risen to a shrill squeak
and she spins frantically about to a new position at DL.]*

ALICE. Have you cut your finger?

WHITE QUEEN. I haven't **yet**, but I soon shall. Oh, oh, oh, **oh!**

ALICE. *[Suppressing a smile]* When?

WHITE QUEEN. *[With a groan]* When I fasten my shawl again.
The pin will come undone. Oh, oh! *[She clutches wildly at
the pin and tries to fasten it.]*

ALICE. You're holding it all crooked! *[Too late. The pin has
slipped and the QUEEN has hurt her finger.]*

WHITE QUEEN. *[With a smile]* You see! That accounts for
the bleeding! Now you understand the way things happen
here.

ALICE. But why don't you scream **now?**

WHITE QUEEN. *[Happily]* I've done all the screaming already.
What would be the good of doing it all over again? *[Stage
lights have been gradually brightening.]*

ALICE. I'm glad it's getting lighter. I thought night was coming
on.

WHITE QUEEN. I wish I could manage to be glad! You must be very happy, being glad whenever you like!

ALICE. *[Suddenly on the verge of tears]* I am. Only it's so **very** different here! That makes me sad.

WHITE QUEEN. *[Hugging ALICE]* Don't go on like that! Consider what a long way you've come today. Really, you've done very well! Consider what o'clock it is. Consider anything, only don't cry.

ALICE. *[Laughing through her tears]* Can **you** keep from crying by considering things?

WHITE QUEEN. *[With friendly determination]* Nobody can do two things at once, you know. Let's consider your age to begin with – how old are you?

ALICE. Seven and a half exactly.

WHITE QUEEN. I'm just one hundred and one, five months and a day.

ALICE. I can't believe **that!**

WHITE QUEEN. *[Piteously]* Can't you?

ALICE. *[Laughing]* I can't believe impossible things.

WHITE QUEEN. You haven't had much practice. When I was your age, I believed as many as six impossible things before breakfast. *[Her shawl is slipping off.]* There goes the shawl again! *[She clutches it in triumph.]* I've got it! Now you shall see me pin it on again, all by myself!

ALICE. Then I hope your finger is better now?

WHITE QUEEN. Oh, much better. Much better! Better – be-etter! Bread-and better, Better-and-bread, bread-and-butter . . .

[Whirling wildly, as the wind surges up again, she disappears off L as the lights dim out. Then exits DL.]

ALICE. Wait please, I need directions.

[ALICE follows her off. Once again in dim red light, we see the procession of pursuers cross the stage from DR to

DL. Just before they disappear into the wings, the QUEEN OF HEARTS pauses and speaks to the KING.]

QUEEN OF HEARTS. Don't let that girl reach the eighth square! I'm determined that she shall not be crowned a queen.

KING OF HEARTS. I won't, my love, I won't.

QUEEN OF HEARTS. Then stir your stumps!

Adventure 13: Humpty Dumpty

[Chessboard drop lifts to reveal HUMPTY DUMPTY sitting on his wall painted like a chessboard. ALICE goes to present herself.]

ALICE. It's Humpty Dumpty! And he's exactly like an egg!

HUMPTY. It's **very** provoking to be called an egg – very.

ALICE. I said you **looked** like an egg, sir. And some eggs are very pretty, you know.

HUMPTY. And some people have no more sense than a baby!

ALICE.   Humpty Dumpty sat on a wall:
                  Humpty Dumpty had a great fall.
                  All the King's horses and all the King's men
                  Couldn't put Humpty Dumpty together again.'

That last line is much too long for the poetry.

HUMPTY. Don't stand chattering to yourself. Tell me your name and your business.

ALICE. My **name** is Alice, and I'm crossing the chessboard to become a queen.

HUMPTY. Alice is a stupid name. What does it mean?

ALICE. **Must** a name mean something?

HUMPTY. Of course. **My** name means the shape I am . . . and a handsome shape it is too. With a name like yours, you might be any shape.

ALICE. Why do you sit here all alone?

HUMPTY. Why, because there's nobody with me! Did you think I didn't know the answer to **that**? Ask me another.

ALICE. Don't you think you'd be safer down on the ground?

HUMPTY. What easy riddles you ask! Of course, I don't think so. If ever I **did** fall off . . . which there's no chance of . . . **The King has promised with his very own mouth . . . to . . .**

ALICE. To send all his horses and all his men.

HUMPTY. *[Annoyed]* You've been listening at doors . . . and keyhole.

ALICE. I haven't either. It's in a book. *[Changing the subject]* What a beautiful belt you've got on! At least, a beautiful bow tie . . . no, a belt, I think – *[Aside]* If only I knew which was neck, and which was waist!

HUMPTY. *[Very angry]* It's a **most provoking** thing when a person doesn't know a bow tie from a belt!

ALICE. *[Humbly]* I'm sorry.

HUMPTY. *[Relenting]* It's a tie, child. It's a present from the White Queen. There now!

ALICE. Is it really?

HUMPTY. She gave it to me – for an **un**-birthday present.

ALICE. *[Puzzled]* I beg your pardon?

HUMPTY. I'm not offended.

ALICE. I mean, what **is** an un-birthday present?

HUMPTY. A present given when it **isn't** your birthday.

ALICE. I like birthday presents best.

HUMPTY. You don't know what you're talking about. How many days are there in a year?

ALICE. Three hundred and sixty-five.

HUMPTY. And how many birthdays have you?

ALICE. One.

HUMPTY. And if you take one from three hundred and sixty-five, what remains?

ALICE. Three hundred and sixty-four, of course.

HUMPTY. That shows that there are three hundred and sixty-four days when you might get un-birthday presents. There's glory for you!

ALICE. I don't know what you mean by 'glory.'

HUMPTY. *[Contemptuously]* Of course you don't – till I tell you. I meant 'there's a nice knock-down argument for you!'

ALICE. But 'glory' doesn't mean 'a nice knock-down argument.'

HUMPTY. When I use a word, it means just what I choose it to mean – neither more nor less.

ALICE. The question is, whether you **can** make words mean so many different things.

HUMPTY. The question is which is to be master, that's all. Impenetrability! That's what I say!

ALICE. You seem to be very clever at explaining words, sir. Could you tell me the meaning of a poem called 'Jabberwocky?'

HUMPTY. I could if I choose. I can explain all the poems that ever were invented, and a good many that haven't been invented yet. But instead I'm going to give you a piece of advice.

ALICE. Thank you.

HUMPTY. This is important, so listen carefully.

> 'I sent a message to the fish.
> I told them, 'This is what I wish.'
> The little fishes' answer was
> 'We cannot do it, sir, **because** . . .'

[Stops reciting]

ALICE. *[After brief pause]* That's your **advice?**

HUMPTY. The important part is coming. *[Resumes]*

> Then someone came to me and said,
> 'The little fishes are in bed.'
> I took a corkscrew from the shelf;
> I went to wake them up myself.
> And when I found the door was locked,
> I pulled and pushed and kicked and knocked.
> And when I found the door was shut,
> I tried to turn the handle, but . . .

ALICE. *[A very long pause]* Is that all?

HUMPTY. And so my advice is ... *[Suddenly urgent]* Run!

ALICE. I beg your pardon?

HUMPTY. Run! Run for your life! It's the Queen of Hearts! Run! *[He's so excited that he falls backward off the wall, with a great crash.]*

ALICE. The Queen of Hearts!

[The QUEEN OF HEARTS rushes on with her followers. The chessboard drop closes to cover tableau stage.]

QUEEN OF HEARTS. There she is! Off with her head! Off with her head! *[Lights dim down]*

Adventure 14: Alice's coronation.

[A blare of trumpets. Lights brighten DL as the RED and WHITE QUEENS enter.]

RED QUEEN. I command you, stop!

WHITE QUEEN. I command you, stop!

QUEEN OF HEARTS. Off with her head!

ALICE. What can I do?

RABBIT. Alice, **stand perfectly still!** *[ALICE freezes. A drum rolls. On one side, the QUEEN OF HEARTS and her EXECU-TIONER advance slowly in silence. On the other, the RED AND WHITE QUEENS advance, holding bundles.]*

ALICE. Help!

RABBIT. Stand still! *[The QUEEN OF HEARTS reaches ALICE. The QUEEN OF HEARTS gestures, and her EXECUTIONER raises his axe. Then the RED QUEEN unfolds a velvet cape and drapes it over ALICE'S shoulders, and the WHITE QUEEN sets a royal crown on ALICE'S head. Trumpets blare.]*

RED AND WHITE QUEENS. All hail, Queen Alice!
QUEEN OF HEARTS. What?
ALL. All hail, Queen Alice!
RABBIT. Hip, hip —
ALL. Hooray!
QUEEN OF HEARTS. Wait a minute . . .
RABBIT. Hip, hip —
ALL. Hooray!
ALICE. Am I really Queen? This must be the eighth square.
QUEEN OF HEARTS. No.
RED QUEEN. Yes! You crossed the chessboard.
WHITE QUEEN. And you can do what you wish.
ALICE. Well, this is grand. I never thought I'd get to be Queen.
    If I really am a Queen.
RED QUEEN. *[Politely, to WHITE QUEEN]* I invite you to
    Alice's dinner-party this afternoon.
WHITE QUEEN. *[To RED QUEEN]* And I invite **you**, Your
    Majesty.
ALICE. I didn't know I was to have a party at all, but if there is
    to be one, shouldn't I invite the guests?
RED QUEEN. The guests have already been invited and we must
    hurry, before they fall asleep!
WHITE QUEEN. I know just how they feel. *[Sighs deeply and
    rests her head on ALICE'S shoulder]* I am so sleepy!
RED QUEEN. She's tired, poor thing! Smooth her hair — lend
    her your nightcap — sing her a soothing lullaby.
ALICE. *[Smooths the WHITE QUEEN'S hair]* I haven't got a
    nightcap with me, and I don't know any soothing lullabies.
RABBIT. Oh, my ears and whiskers! We shall all be late! Come
    along, Your Royal Majesties.

*[The upstage curtains open. A banquet table has been
brought on and seated behind it are as many of the cast
as can be crowded onto the platform. Prominent to be*

seen are the KING OF HEARTS, the MAD HATTER, the
MARCH HARE, the DORMOUSE, the TWEEDLE brothers,
etc. They are eating and drinking merrily.]

QUEEN OF HEARTS. We've missed the soup and fish. Bring
on the mutton! *[Raising her goblet, as ALICE and the*
others arrive at the table.] I drink to Queen Alice's health!

ALL. Queen Alice's health!

QUEEN OF HEARTS. Well, my girl, I did my best to catch up
with you. I was hot on your heels from square to square. I
had planned to chop off your head before you ever set a
crown on it. But it's too late to remedy matters now. So
you may go safely home whenever you like.

RED QUEEN. Now we all drank to **your** health, you ought to
return thanks in a neat little speech. *[The following can*
be set to music, or chanted as choric speech.]

ALICE. *[Raising her glass]*

> To the Looking-Glass World, now let it be said,
> I've a scepter in hand, I've a crown on my head,
> Let the Wonderland Creatures, whatever they be,
> Come and dine with the Red Queen, the White
> Queen and me!

ALL. *[Join in]*

> Then fill up the glasses as quick as you can,
> And sprinkle the table with buttons and bran.
> Put cats in the coffee, and mice in the tea . . .
> And welcome Queen Alice with thirty-times-three!
> With thirty-times-three!
> With thirty-times-three!
> And welcome Queen Alice with thirty-times-three!

ALICE.

> O Looking-Glass creatures, I beg you draw near!
> 'Tis an honor to have you, a favor to hear.

'Tis a privilege high to have dinner and tea
Along with the Red Queen, the White Queen and me!

ALL.

So fill up the glasses with syrup and ink,
And anything else that is pleasant to drink.
Mix sand with the cider, and wool with the wine . . .
And welcome Queen Alice with ninety-times-nine!
With ninety-times-nine!
With ninety-times-nine!
And welcome Queen Alice with ninety-times-nine!

*[As the chorus ends, the group at the banquet table freeze
into a tableau and the lights dim very slowly. ALICE comes
forward to DC where a pinspot irises in on her.]*

ALICE. I know that soon I shall wake up in my chair by the
fireside with a small black kitten in my lap and realize that
everything that happened was all a dream. But I can never —
not ever — as long as I live — forget my magical visit to
Wonderland. *[The spotlight goes out.]*

[CURTAIN]

PRODUCTION NOTES

COSTUMES: It is suggested that the actors wear tights, leotards, and colored T-shirts, the typical dance company rehearsal garments. To this basic outfit may be added capes, sashes, scarves, tabards, tunics, et cetera. The costumer should be guided by the illustrations of Sir John Tenniel, with particular emphasis on the headdresses, wigs, and masks to suggest the famous characters.

SCENERY: Scenery should be as simple and imaginative as possible, relying chiefly on lighting effects. The basic set and various scene changes are quite fully described in the body of the play. Some additional suggestions and thoughts are presented here.

SETTING: A large bare stage draped, if possible, and painted black, if it's convenient. Half-way upstage is a center-opening Traveler curtain. Behind the Traveler is a smaller, raised platform that acts as the Tableau Stage. Exit stairs are placed on either upstage end of the Tableau Platform and the downstage edge is either a ramp or additional stairs.

A small sky-drop (an additional small curtain) hangs upstage of the Tableau Platform. Green plastic, or gauze, may be unrolled and brought in front of Alice and the Mouse by stagehands in Wonderland costumes for the underwater scene. It's also possible to use a green gauze drop for this. A rolling drop may be rigged at the downstage end of the Tableau Platform and painted a bold red and white checkerboard pattern.

The Traveler opens and closes, or the lights dim down, or the checkerboard drop raises and lowers, to reveal new scenes. All other scenery can be lightweight cutouts and may be carried on by cast members and positioned. Small platforms which roll on from a nearby offstage position can also fill out the scenery for each new adventure.

68

PRODUCTION NOTES (cont.)

SET PIECES
Act I

1. ALICE'S TREE: Alice's tree on tableau platform. A small gold table stands DL, hung on wires to grid. Table has crepepaper accordion legs with weighted feet, so that it will appear to grow taller when lifted. Suggest velcro tabs on tabletop and bottom of bottle for safety.

2. THE POOL OF TEARS: Green plastic or gauze rolled out in front of the tableau platform, with a rock cutout UC agitated to imitate water.

3. ON A MUSHROOM: A rolling mushroom platform appears DR, with breakaway edge for Alice to 'eat.'

4. HOUSE OF THE DUCHESS: A rolling door-flat with practical stoop. Full kitchen on Tableau Stage with boxy stove, rocking chair, electric paper-lantern 'Cheshire Cat' face with internal lighting and painted eyes and grin.

5. IN A TREE: A standing tree or leafy bough hung on wires, with a second electric Cheshire Cat. This one has a body and tail. It is wired for two dimmers, one to light face and body, the other to light grin; all located UR.

6. TEA PARTY: Tea table DL set with many places and many chairs.

Act II

7. CROQUET COURT: A garden on the tableau stage, with large central rose tree. Most roses are white and a few red. Three stepladders stand around the tree.

69

PRODUCTION NOTES (cont.)

8.   ON A BEACH: A seaside scene on Tableau Stage, with large seashells and a leaning beach umbrella.

9.   THE THRONE ROOM: Two red thrones under a canopy painted playing-card style, on the Tableau Stage. Witness box freestanding DL.

Act III

10.   THE CHESSBOARD — RED QUEEN: The traveller curtain is open, but the Tableau Stage is hidden by a smaller drop curtain with large red and white chessboard squares.

11.   CHESSBOARD — TWEEDLEDUM AND TWEEDLEDEE: Chessboard drop.

12.   CHESSBOARD — WHITE QUEEN: Chessboard drop.

13.   CHESSBOARD — HUMPTY DUMPTY: A painted chessboard wall on Tableau Stage, with mattress hidden behind to catch Humpty's fall.

14.   CORONATION OF ALICE: Chessboard drop returns; then chessboard drop lifts revealing red and white checkerboard banquet table with many chairs facing audience.

PROPERTIES (Listed by scene)

Act I

1.   Book; bottle with DRINK ME tag; large pocket watch; white gloves; executioner's axe; handkerchief with plastic bag and wet sponge for 'tears.'

2.   Hookah or water pipe.

PRODUCTION NOTES (cont.)

4.   Large envelope with Q monogram on it; pepper shaker; spoon and pot of soup; baby doll with pig face and blanket; miscellaneous pots and pans, frisbee 'plates.'

6.   Large teapot, cups, saucers, pocket watch.

Act II

7.   Three red paintbrushes, three red paintbuckets, two spears, axe, two 'flamingo' croquet mallets.

8.   Handkerchief; two spears; chain with cardboard 'wrist manacles.'

9.   Chain with cardboard 'wrist menacles;' small table with tart exhibit; scroll; axe; mock heraldic trumpets with banners; teacup, bread and butter; several quills and writing-boards; several decks of playing cards.

Act III

10.   Hand mirror with cord; small book; two large biscuits; tape measure; axe; two spears.

11.   Two handkerchiefs; beach umbrella.

12.   White shawl, adhesive tape and gauze bandage; brooch; axe; two spears.

13.   Two spears; heraldic trumpets.

14.   Velvet cape; royal crown; pocket watch; dishes; wine-glasses; forks and spoons; candelabra.

HOW DOTH THE LITTLE CROCODILE

Lewis Carroll

Hymn-like

How doth the lit - tle cro - co - dile im -
prove his shi - ning tail ——— And pour the wa - ters
of the Nile on ev - 'ry gol - den scale. How cheer-ful-ly he
seems to grin, how neat - ly spreads his claws. And
wel - comes lit - tle fish - es in with gent - ly smi - ling jaws.

WILL YOU WALK A LITTLE FASTER?

Lewis Carroll

Politely

'Will you walk a lit - tle fas - ter?' said a whi-ting to a snail; There's a
'You can real-ly have no no-tion how de-light-ful it will be— When they

por-poise right be-hind me and he's tread - ing on my tail. See how
take us up and throw us, with you lob - sters out to sea! But the

ea - ger - ly the lob - sters and the tur - tles all ad-vance!— They are
snail re - plied, 'Too far, too far!' and gave a look as-kance. — Said he

wait-ing on the shin - gle, Will you come and join the dance?
thank'd the whi-ting kind-ly, But he would not join the dance.

Will you, won't you, will you, won't you, will you join the dance?
Would not, could not, would not, could not, would not join the dance?

Will you, won't you, will you, won't you, won't you join the dance?'
Would not, could not, would not, could not, could not join the dance.

BEAUTIFUL SOUP

74

beau - ti - ful, beau - ti - ful soup!

'TIS THE VOICE OF THE LOBSTER

[Optional]

Lewis Carroll

Sensibly

'Tis the voice of the lob - ster,' I heard him de - clare; You have bak'd me too brown, I must su-gar my hair' As a duck with its eye-lids, so he with his nose, trims his belt and his but-tons, and turns out his toes. When the sands are all dry, he is gay as a lark, and will talk in con - temp-tu-ous tones of the shark: But when the tide ri-ses and

sharks are a - round, his — voice has a ti-mid and tre-mu-lous sound.

voice has a ti - mid and tre - mu - lous sound.

This work is published by Samuel French, an imprint of Concord Theatricals Corp.

No one shall make any changes in this title(s) for the purpose of production. No part of this book may be reproduced, stored in a retrieval system, scanned, uploaded, or transmitted in any form, by any means, now known or yet to be invented, including mechanical, electronic, digital, photocopying, recording, videotaping, or otherwise, without the prior written permission of the publisher. No one shall share this title(s), or any part of this title(s), through any social media or file hosting websites.

For all inquiries regarding motion picture, television, online/digital and other media rights, please contact Concord Theatricals Corp.

MUSIC AND THIRD-PARTY MATERIALS USE NOTE

Licensees are solely responsible for obtaining formal written permission from copyright owners to use copyrighted music and/or other copyrighted third-party materials (e.g., artworks, logos) in the performance of this play and are strongly cautioned to do so. If no such permission is obtained by the licensee, then the licensee must use only original music and materials that the licensee owns and controls. Licensees are solely responsible and liable for clearances of all third-party copyrighted materials, including without limitation music, and shall indemnify the copyright owners of the play(s) and their licensing agent, Concord Theatricals Corp., against any costs, expenses, losses and liabilities arising from the use of such copyrighted third-party materials by licensees. For music, please contact the appropriate music licensing authority in your territory for the rights to any incidental music.

IMPORTANT BILLING AND CREDIT REQUIREMENTS

If you have obtained performance rights to this title, please refer to your licensing agreement for important billing and credit requirements.

Ingram Content Group UK Ltd.
Milton Keynes UK
UKHW022235080323
418264UK00012B/682